the yellowhorse discovery

Tami Brumbaugh

BEACON HILL PRESS
OF KANSAS CITY

Copyright 2009
by Beacon Hill Press of Kansas City

Printed in the United States of America

ISBN 978-0-8341-2413-4

Cover Design: Doug Bennett
Illustrator: Paula Becker
Inside Design: Sharon Page

Editor: Donna Manning
Assistant Editors: Kimberly Adams and
Laura Lohberger

Note: This fictional story is based on the author's child-hood experiences while living with her family on the campus of the Nazarene Indian Bible College. It is part of the *Kidz Passport to Missions* curriculum.

10 9 8 7 6 5 4 3 2 1

Dedication

To the Native American children who rang my doorbell each day to play. And to my parents, Gene Cope (Director of Campus Development) and Karen Cope (Administrative Secretary), who followed God's call to work at the Nazarene Indian Bible College.

Contents

1

The Great Chase

"Jodi, please keep your younger brothers and sisters out of the house," Mother instructed. "And hold Jack," she said, as she pushed a squirming young child into Jodi's arms.

"But Mom," Jodi complained, "Aaron and I want to walk around and . . ."

"There'll be time for that later!" Mother snapped. Her frown softened. "I'm sorry, Jodi. Our trip to Albuquerque [AL-buh-ker-kee], New Mexico has been a long one. Your dad and I are tired. But we must move our things into the house. I won't make you watch the young ones much longer.

"Aaron, I need your help too," Mother said. At his feet, she set two matching cradleboards filled with sleeping twins. The flat boards created tiny, wooden beds. They had leather straps that wrapped around the babies to hold them in place.

Aaron grinned. "They won't be much trouble," he thought.

"Oh, and please watch the others too,"
Mother added. She sat their five-year-old sister
by Jodi and their three-year-old brother by
Aaron. But as quickly as Mother sat the three-
year-old down, he hopped up and ran.

"This is going to get old quick," moaned
Aaron, chasing after his brother.

Jodi slipped off her worn sandals and began drawing pictures in the sand with her toes.
She giggled as she watched Aaron chase their
brother past several houses. Aaron caught him
just before he ran into the long sword-shaped
leaves of a yucca [YUK-uh] plant. Then they
raced past a gym and a small church before finally returning.

"Now sit!" Aaron firmly told his brother, as
he tried to catch his breath.

"I thought we were going to look around
the school grounds together," Jodi said, laugh-
ing. "It looks like you've already seen every-
thing."

"Since I was trying to keep up with him,"
Aaron said, pointing at his brother, "I didn't see
anything!"

The children watched as their parents carried heavy boxes from their old blue truck into

their house. As they were struggling to pick up a mattress, a white man with black hair and a beard hurried up to them.

"Welcome! My name is Gene Cope. I work here at the Nazarene Indian Bible College."

Dad responded, "We're the Yellowhorse family from the Navajo [NAV-uh-hoh] Reservation. I'm here to attend classes."

"Let me help you unload your truck," offered Gene. Together they moved the rest of their belongings inside.

"I know your family will be crowded in this one-bedroom house," Gene said. "But it's the only house we have empty. A Work and Witness team is coming to build two three-bedroom houses. As soon they get one built, you can move into it."

Mother's eyes widened. "We've never had more than one bedroom!"

Jodi elbowed Aaron and smiled. She loved the idea of everyone not having to sleep in the same room.

Just then, several dark-skinned children began running and pointing toward the road. "They're here! They're here!" they yelled.

2

I Spy

A cloud of dust surrounded two white vans as they parked in front of the college office building.

"That's the Work and Witness team," Gene told Mr. Yellowhorse. "I'd better show them where to go. If you need anything, come to the office." Gene turned his attention to the children surrounding him. "This is the Yellowhorse family. Can you tell them hello?" he asked, as he headed toward the vans.

"Hi," a young Apache [uh-PA-chee] boy said.

"Ya at eeh [YAH et ay] (hello)," said two young Navajo girls.

The children were curious about the new family. They studied them for a few moments, then scampered off toward the office.

"Dad, can Aaron and I look around?" asked Jodi.

"Yes, but be back before it gets dark."

11

Jodi and Aaron raced to the nearest building and peeked around the corner. The man with the beard was still talking to one of the van drivers. The children they had just met were hopping up and down around him. He pointed toward the gym, and the driver climbed back into the van.

"Where are they going?" asked Aaron.

"Let's follow them," Jodi answered.

They ran from building to building, hiding around the corner of each one.

"I hope we can find our way home," Aaron said. "These buildings all look the same."

"You're right," said Jodi. She looked around at all of the tan-colored buildings. They were covered with stucco [STUH-koh], a mixture of cement, sand, and lime.

Jodi and Aaron watched as the vans pulled up to the gym and stopped again. Jodi counted 14 white people who climbed out of the vans. They were all adults, except for one young boy.

"He doesn't look much older than us," said Aaron. "How old do you think he is?"

"Um . . . maybe a teenager," answered Jodi. "Hey, look! They're carrying in their stuff."

The team members unloaded their suitcas-

es first. Then they began carrying in cardboard boxes. The boy dropped one of the boxes, and clothing spilled out.

"Wow!" Jodi exclaimed. "They sure have a lot of stuff. I wonder if all those clothes are for them."

"I hope not," Aaron answered. "That boy is picking up dresses. And I don't see anyone in their group who would wear a dress."

As the boy placed the last piece of clothing in the box, he looked up. Suddenly, he smiled and waved.

"Oh, no. He saw us," Jodi whispered.

Jodi and Aaron gave a slight wave. Then they quickly turned and ran back to their new home.

3

The View from a Jungle Gym

The next morning, Jodi woke up to the sound of crying twins. She pulled the blanket over her ears. Her five-year-old sister pulled the blanket back in her direction.

"I'm afraid, Jodi," she said, trembling. "What if our friends back home forget about us?"

Jodi tried to comfort her sister. "They won't forget about us. And we'll make new friends. You'll see."

Jodi stroked her sister's black hair. "Remember, Grandma is coming to see us soon. And we can go and visit her too."

Just then, Mother walked into the room bouncing one of the twins on her hip. "After we eat, you can go outside and play," she said. "Maybe you'll see the children we met yesterday. They seemed friendly."

The family squeezed around a little table in the kitchen. In front of each older child, Mother set a tortilla [tor-TEE-yuh] (a round, flat bread made with cornmeal or flour). She topped each tortilla with potato, egg, and a little meat. The children rolled up their tortillas and enjoyed the familiar meal.

"Where's Dad?" asked Jodi.

"He went to the office to sign up for classes. And he's going to look for a job too. I hope he can find something near the school."

Jodi loved being with her father now. He had really changed. Earlier in the summer, he met a friend who had attended the Nazarene Indian Bible College. The friend told him about the school and what he had learned. Jodi's dad began talking about someone named Jesus, and he started going to church. Soon, her dad seemed much happier. Then he learned there were students at the college from Indian tribes, including the Navajo. He decided to go to the Bible college too.

"Do you think when Dad has learned more

about Jesus, he'll tell us about Him?" asked Jodi. "Or are we too young to learn about Jesus?"

"I don't know, Jodi," Mother answered. "I'm just beginning to learn about Him myself."

Jodi and Aaron dug through their clothes until they found enough jeans and T-shirts to dress everyone. Once dressed, Jodi brushed and braided her long, black hair. Then she and Aaron headed toward the door.

"Can you take the little ones out to play?" Mother asked. "I think there's a playground around here."

"All of them?" Aaron frowned.

"I'll keep the twins," Mother offered.

The children soon found an old merry-go-round and a wooden jungle gym to climb. Aaron climbed to the top of the ladder.

"Hey, Jodi," he called, "I can see the Work and Witness team from up here!"

Jodi wasted no time climbing up the ladder too. "I see the boy who waved at us yesterday. What is he doing?"

"It looks like he's hammering nails into something. He's working as hard as the grown-ups."

"Harder than you, that's for sure," Jodi

17

teased. "It looks like they're building a house. I wonder if that's our new house. Just imagine! *Three* bedrooms! Hey, Jack! Take that out of your mouth!"

Jodi quickly climbed down the ladder and removed a rock from her baby brother's mouth. Jodi and Aaron decided they had better take turns watching the Work and Witness team.

The children played until they saw their mother. "Kids! Come quick!" she called. "Your dad is home, and he has good news!"

4
An Accident

"What's the good news?" asked Aaron. He and the others crowded around their mom and dad.

"I got a job right here at the college," Dad said, hugging all of the children he could reach. "There's a classroom where students make Native American pottery. I showed several people here my artwork, and they like it. They've agreed to let me make and paint the pottery they sell."

Mother beamed. "Isn't that great?"

"I knew God would provide for us," Dad said.

Jodi was happy, yet confused. "I thought God was in heaven. How could He give you a job here?"

"It's hard to explain." Dad patted her on the head. "You'll understand when you're older."

Jodi wanted to understand now, but she did not ask anymore questions.

"Let's celebrate!" said Mother. "I'll fix some mutton (sheep) stew."

After lunch, the younger children crawled into bed to take a nap. Jodi and Aaron went in search of the Work and Witness team. But the only team member they could find was the boy. He was sitting on the concrete floor of the house picking up scattered nails. Jodi and her brother stood a short distance away, silently watching him.

As the boy placed the last nail into a box and shut the lid, Aaron coughed. It scared the boy, and he nearly dropped the box of nails.

"Hello," the boy said, standing up. "My name is Brandon."

"Hi. I'm Jodi. And this is my brother, Aaron."

"Do you live at the Nazarene Indian Bible College?" asked Brandon.

"Yes," Jodi answered. "We just moved in yesterday. Our dad will be going to school and working here."

"Are you part of the Yellowhorse family?" Brandon asked. "We were told this home would be for a new family with lots of kids."

"That's us," Aaron answered. "I can't believe this big house is for our family."

"It is," Brandon said, smiling. "We got a lot done today. But now the team is in a meeting. While I'm waiting, do you want to look around?"

"Yes!" exclaimed Aaron and Jodi.

Brandon pointed out where each room would be in the house. "We will finish the walls in a day or two."

"How do you know about building houses?" Aaron asked.

"My dad is a carpenter. I go with him on Saturdays and watch him work."

"Why are you the only kid on the team?" asked Jodi.

"I got to come because my dad is the team leader, and my mom is in charge of the cooking. But I'm not just tagging along. I like to work," Brandon said.

"We know. Every time we see the team, you're working as hard as the rest." Jodi blushed as she realized that now Brandon knew they had been spying on the team.

"We're just curious," Jodi explained. "We've never heard of a Work and Witness team before."

"A Work and Witness team helps other

people by doing work, like building these homes," explained Brandon. "And the teams tell people about Jesus."

"Jesus? We've heard of Him," Jodi said. "He is the reason we came here. Our dad wants to learn more about Him. But how do you know about Jesus? I thought we were too young to know Him."

"Everyone can know Jesus," said Brandon. "He loves children too. You can read about Him in the Bible. Do you have a Bible?"

"Dad might have one, but we don't," Aaron said.

"Our team brought a box full of Bibles. We can go get one for you right now, if you want."

"Really? I would love that!" Jodi exclaimed.

"Me too!" said Aaron.

As Aaron jumped up, he bumped into a tall ladder that rested against a wall.

"Oh, no!" shouted Jodi.

5

The Rescue

Aaron's mouth dropped open as he watched the ladder crash into another wall. "I'm sorry! Did I ruin the house? Can I help you fix it?"

Brandon looked up. "It's OK. The ladder only loosened a board. I can pound the nails back down."

He set the ladder against a nearby wall and carefully climbed to the top. He tried to reach the loose nails above him, but he was too far away.

"What are you going to do now?" Aaron asked.

"I'll just have to climb onto the roof and hammer the nails from the top."

"The roof! Is that safe?" Jodi questioned.

"I helped my dad do it once before," Brandon said. He climbed onto the roof and began walking across the boards.

Jodi twisted her braid nervously, while Aaron held his breath.

Brandon successfully bent down and hammered in the nails. "There. See? It's OK."

But as Brandon stood up, he lost his balance and began to fall. On his way down, he caught hold of a board and dangled high above Jodi and Aaron's heads.

"Hold on!" Jodi screamed. She grabbed the ladder and tried to drag it close to Brandon's feet. But she could not. The ladder was too heavy.

"I can't hold on much longer!" Brandon yelled. "Dear Jesus, help me!"

"Aaron, help me!" screamed Jodi.

Aaron grabbed the ladder and started pulling. Jodi pushed with all her might. Just as his hands began to slip, Brandon· managed to slide his foot on a step. Aaron steadied the ladder as Brandon grabbed for the sides and got his other foot on the step. He climbed down and sank to the ground, trembling.

"Whew!" Brandon let out a sigh. "That was a close one," he said, rubbing his sore arms.

"Too close!" Jodi agreed.

"I should have let my dad fix the board. I

just wanted to prove that I can help our team."
Brandon closed his eyes and prayed, "Thank
You, God, for protecting us. I love You."

For a while, they all sat on the ground
without saying a word.

Finally, Aaron said, "Brandon, how about
those Bibles?"

6

Two Special Gifts

"Dad! Look!" Jodi and Aaron called, as they rushed into the pottery room.

"Where did you get the Bibles?" Dad asked.

"Brandon gave them to us," Jodi said.

"Who's Brandon?"

"The boy who's with the Work and Witness team," explained Aaron. "We met him today at the house they're building for us. He almost fell off the roof! But we moved the ladder and helped him get down."

"He almost fell off the roof?" Dad nearly dropped the vase he was painting. "Why was he on the roof?"

"It's a long story, Dad," Jodi said. "But we're all fine. Brandon gave us these Bibles and told us about Jesus. He told us that Jesus is for kids too. We've already read a Bible story from a book called Matthew."

Dad set his vase on the table and smiled. "I thought you were too young to understand. It looks like we can learn about Jesus together. I'm glad Brandon talked to you. I'd like to meet this young man."

"He's just a kid, Dad," Aaron said. "Like us."

"I guess God can use kids too," Dad replied.

Later that week, everyone at the Nazarene Indian Bible College helped to prepare a going-away dinner for the Work and Witness team. The smell of fry bread (tortilla-shaped bread that is fried) filled the cafeteria [kaf-uh-TIR-ee-uh].

Jodi and Aaron showed Brandon how to eat Navajo tacos. They covered the fry bread with layers of beans, meat, cheddar cheese, lettuce, tomatoes, and salsa [SAHL-suh] (a spicy tomato sauce). Jodi used a fork to eat her taco. Aaron rolled his up and took huge bites.

"This is great!" Brandon exclaimed after taking a huge bite, like Aaron.

Just then, several young girls ran through the cafeteria. They were wearing the dresses that had spilled from the box Brandon carried earlier.

"Did the Work and Witness team bring those dresses?" asked Jodi.

Brandon nodded. "We brought a lot of clothes for the students and their families. There may be something you can wear too."

Jodi smiled. "I would like to have a dress," she said.

After dinner, people thanked the team for their help. Jodi and Aaron gave Brandon a special brown paper bag.

"Open it," Aaron said.

Brandon reached in and pulled out a small vase. It was painted in red, orange, and black Native American designs.

"Wow! It's amazing!" Brandon exclaimed. He ran his fingers over its smooth finish.

"Our dad made it just for you," Jodi explained.

"Thanks. Now I have something to help me remember you and this Work and Witness trip. But I don't have anything to give you."

Jodi smiled. "You gave us Bibles and helped us discover that Jesus loves us. That's a great gift!"